FISHING: **TIPS & TECHNIQUES**™

FLY FISHING

SALLY CROCKETT

rosen publishing's
rosen central®

New York

For Daddy Boy and Uncle Boo

Published in 2012 by The Rosen Publishing Group, Inc.
29 East 21st Street, New York, NY 10010

Copyright © 2012 by The Rosen Publishing Group, Inc.

First Edition

Library of Congress Cataloging-in-Publication Data

Crockett, Sally.
Fly fishing / Sally Crockett.—1st ed.
    p. cm.—(Fishing: tips & techniques)
Includes bibliographical references and index.
ISBN 978-1-4488-4601-6 (library binding)
ISBN 978-1-4488-4606-1 (pbk.)
ISBN 978-1-4488-4737-2 (6-pack)
1. Fly fishing—Juvenile literature. I. Title.
SH456.C76 2012
799.12'4—dc22

2010048421

Manufactured in Malaysia

CPSIA Compliance Information: Batch #S11YA: For further information, contact Rosen Publishing, New York, New York, at 1-800-237-9932.

CONTENTS

Welcome to the wonderful world of fly fishing, a sport that takes just hours to learn but a lifetime to master. If you're a beginner, nothing could be easier than to pick up a rod, learn a few basics, and head out to the water. You'll have a lot of fun, and you might even catch a few fish. But if you get "hooked," you could spend decades perfecting your technique and learning the infinite subtleties of fly fishing.

When most people think about fly fishing, they imagine fishing for trout in a mountain stream. But fly fishing techniques can be used to hook lots of different types of fish in exotic locations across the globe. You can fish for bass in an Ozark lake, for steelhead in Oregon rivers, for barracuda in the Gulf of Mexico, or for salmon along the Pacific coast.

Given the wide range of possibilities regarding types of fish and fishing locations, just what is fly fishing? The simple answer is that fly fishing is the art of hooking fish through trickery. In normal fishing, an angler uses bait—such as a live worm—to catch fish. But fly fishermen use a different strategy. They choose a handcrafted fly designed to imitate

4

the fish's favorite meal, cast it out onto the water, and move it around to make it seem lifelike. When a fish is fooled by this performance, the angler hooks it.

Fly fishing is a great way to learn about nature. Good anglers learn all they can about the spot where they are fishing: what the fish in those waters eat, how they behave in different seasons, what entices them, and what frightens them. Fly fishing provides the angler with the opportunity to understand his or her environment from the inside out. It teaches problem solving: when the fish aren't biting, the angler must figure out why and change his or her approach. Fly fishing also teaches attention to detail. An angler could do a great job tricking the fish, but if he or she didn't tie the leader to the line properly, the fish could become the proverbial "one that got away." Above all, fly fishing teaches patience and perseverance. If at first you don't catch a fish, try, try, again. You'll be that much more proud when all your hard work pays off.

CHAPTER 1

SAFETY AND SPORTSMANSHIP

Before anglers hit the water, they need to make sure that they're on the right side of the law—and that they're fishing safely and responsibly.

Licenses and Rules

Most states require anglers to purchase a fishing license before they start fishing. However, whether an angler needs a license to fish depends on who the angler is and where he or she is planning to fish. For instance, in New York State, children under sixteen can fish for free. Anglers also don't need a license if they're fishing on their own land. Many states hold special events during which no license is needed for a weekend or an entire week. Anglers should take a moment to ask about their state's fishing

In some waters, anglers are required to hold a fishing license. License fees are often used to support conservation efforts, fund hatcheries where fish are raised for release into the wild, and more.

laws at their local bait and tackle shop or research the appropriate laws and regulations on the Internet.

The rules that regulate fishing vary from state to state, from town to town, and from season to season. For instance, on Alabama public rivers, an angler can take home up to five rainbow trout, but no sturgeon. Other spots throughout the country are strictly catch-and-release. Trout fishing season is from March to September in most states, while bass season in most states is from May to February. Fines and other penalties can result from fishing out of season. Regulations about the size and number of fish that anglers can catch can also vary from state to state.

What's the point of all these rules? Fishing laws exist to protect fish populations. Catch limits—putting a cap on the number of fish an angler can pull out of the water in a day—are an important conservation strategy, one that ensures the future viability of fish populations and fishing as a sport and pastime. Just imagine the damage that just a few anglers could wreak if they took all the fish they wanted, day after day! Fishing seasons and size limits are also created with conservation in mind. Fishing seasons often ensure that fish have a chance to spawn in peace. The same is true for size limits. If fish are caught too

Anglers should avoid bunching up when fishing and should leave plenty of space between each other. This makes for safer casting and an increased likelihood of landing fish without getting lines tangled.

young, they won't be able to spawn the next generation. Fishing laws ensure that there will be more fish to catch tomorrow, next week, and in decades to come.

Safety Around Hooks and Rods

Hooks might not look too dangerous, but if you've ever seen somebody take a sharp hook in the eye or neck, you know they can inflict some serious damage. When using sharp hooks, be sure to wear long sleeves, long pants, and close-toed shoes for protection.

If the wind is blowing hard, anglers must watch where they're casting. Take account of the wind strength and direction when deciding where to cast the line. Otherwise, a gust of wind could blow a hook straight into your face or into another person.

Keep a safe distance from other anglers. When fishing with a friend, make sure that you keep clear of his or her casting zone. When relaxing on a boat together, take turns casting, and don't get careless. You don't want to accidentally hook your friend!

Use common sense when stowing fishing gear. Never leave hooks out on the ground streamside or on the floor of a boat. And fishing rods should always be stored upright. This is because stepping on a fishing rod can be just as dangerous as stepping on a rake, only sharp hooks might be involved.

Safety When Wading

One of the great pleasures of fly fishing is wading out into the middle of a stream to cast for trout. Just remember, no matter how deceptively easy wading looks, it can be dangerous. Stream bottoms are often uneven and slippery. It's easy to slip, lose one's balance, and get swept away with the current. That's why it's so important to never, ever wade

It's important to outfit yourself with the right equipment to stay safe and comfortable on the water. This fisherwoman is wearing hip-high waders, helping her stay warm and dry and providing good footing.

out into a stream unless you're a strong swimmer. For these reasons, many anglers wear a life vest when they're fishing in streams, even when they are not in a boat.

If you're wearing hip-high wader boots, don't go into the deep water! You don't want water spilling over the tops of the boots and weighing you down. If you're wearing waders that rise to your chest, don't go near the water without a wader belt. If you slip and fall in the water, the belt will help keep the waders from filling up with water.

Removing a Hook from Skin

No matter how careful anglers are, accidents will happen from time to time. If a fishing hook accidentally gets implanted in the skin, stay calm. If the hook is not barbed, chances are that it can be removed fairly easily.

Take a hand's length of heavy line and string it through the hook's bend. Get a good grip on the line. This line will be used to pull the hook out of the skin. But first, put some pressure on the fly-head area (where the leader is attached to the fly). The skin around the hook will loosen up. That hook cut a path through the skin when it caught on you. You need to get it out along that same path. In one quick, smooth motion, pull on the line and take the hook out.

Obviously, if you hook your eye or neck, or if you can't easily remove the hook yourself, head for the nearest emergency room, stat.

The soles of wader boots are important, too. Most anglers like to match their soles to the type of surface they'll be wading upon. If you're going to be walking on sand and mud, rubber soles with plenty of traction are the way to go. If you'll be wading on gravel or rocks, felt soles will grip the slick algae that grows on rocks and help prevent slipping and sliding. These days, however, there is increasing concern that felt-soled shoes can transport dangerous microorganisms between streams. Boots with metal cleats can be a good alternative to felt-soled boots.

Often when you're wading, you can't get a clear view of the surface in front of you because it's obstructed by rushing water. A wading staff can help you "see" the ground in front of you and provide stability in strong currents. Polarized sunglasses can also cut reflective sun glare and help anglers spot underwater obstacles.

Wading Strategy

Before you start wading, check out the terrain. Decide where you want to fish. What will be the easiest route to get there, and how will you get back? Most important, where will you end up if you get swept away? If the answer is at the bottom of a waterfall on sharp rocks, find a new fishing spot. Period.

It's usually best to start upstream from the spot where you want to stand, then wade across and down to reach the target area. When wading, don't show your face or your back to the current; stand sideways to it. Keep your feet wide apart, and always have one foot firmly planted before you move the next foot. Don't try to climb over big boulders midstream.

If you do fall into the water, stay calm and don't panic. Point your feet downstream and keep your head above water. Ride the current until you reach a safe spot to swim to shore. Fly fishing schools can give further instruction on how to stay safe if caught in rushing water.

This angler has come prepared. He is wearing a hat that protects against the sun's rays, sunglasses to cut glare and protect against UV light, and a life jacket that doubles as a fishing vest. And he has stowed on board a tackle box, a net, and a fishing rod case.

Staying Safe and Healthy on the Water

Safety is even more important when fishing from a boat. Always wear a life vest, and follow all of the boat's safety rules. Check the weather forecast before heading out. And above all, make sure somebody on board knows how to handle the boat safely and according to proper boating rules. Exercise common sense when trying to land fish so that the effort to bring a fish on board doesn't send you or your companions into the water.

Pictured here are some of the most important pieces of an angler's tackle: a rod, reel, and line; a fly box; a landing net; a wicker creel basket, used to keep one's catch fresh; and, of course, a hat for protection from the elements, including the sun.

If you spend all day in the hot sun above a stream that's reflecting ultraviolet (UV) light back up at you, you will get sunburned. Wear sunscreen. Wear a hat. And make sure you always bring your polarized sunglasses. Not only will they cut the glare and help you see through the water, they'll also protect your eyes from light damage that can eventually lead to permanent vision deterioration.

CHAPTER 2

FLY FISHING EQUIPMENT

*T*he vast variety of rods, fishing lines, reels, and flies out there can make choosing the fly fishing gear that's right for you and your needs a daunting task. Understanding the basics of what each piece of tackle is meant to do can help you make an informed decision when it comes time to buy your first fly fishing equipment.

The Fishing Rod

Your first piece of tackle should be a fishing rod. There was a time when all fishing rods were crafted from wood. Then fiberglass rods began to appear. These days most rods are made of graphite, a substance that is both very strong and very flexible. Anglers who really care about tradition can still buy bamboo rods, but these are very expensive.

Every fishing rod is marked with a length and a weight. The length, of course, refers to how long the rod is. The weight reveals what type of line should be used with the rod. So a 9' 6" rod would be a 9-foot- (2.74 meters) long rod, designed for use with 6 weight line. Shorter, lighter people usually fish with shorter, lighter rods. Taller, heavier anglers will generally use more heavy-duty rods.

What you're fishing for partially determines the weight of the rod and fly line. Fly line comes in weights from 1, the lightest, to 12, the heaviest. The lightest lines are used for the smallest fish and the calmest water—for instance, small trout in a gentle stream, where

Different fish species call for different rods, reels, lines, leaders, and flies. Do your homework ahead of time so that you don't try to catch a big fish with a small rod and small line, or vice versa.

a heavy line would frighten fish. The heaviest lines are used for big fish in rough salt waters, where there are strong winds and waves to contend with. Of course, rods designed to cast light line are lighter and more delicate than the monster rods created to hook huge ocean fish.

Anglers also want to consider the action of their rods. "Action" refers to how a rod bends and unbends when casting. Rods with a stiff action don't bend too much, which is good for casting larger, heavier flies. Rods with a soft action are more flexible. Beginners should start with a moderate action rod.

Fly lines come in a wide variety of shapes, sizes, colors, weights, and densities depending on the kind of fish you are trying to land and the kind of water in which you are fishing.

The Reel

Most fly fishing rods and reels are sold separately. The reel is where the line and backing are stored. In fly fishing, the reel doesn't help the angler cast—but it does help him or her retrieve and store the line when the reel's handle is turned. Some reels are designed to retrieve line faster than others. Some even rewind automatically. Reels also provide drag, or resistance. When a strong fish is tugging at the line, drag helps the angler resist the fish's pull. Drag also tires out the fish, making it easier to pull it out of the water.

Fly Line Shape

Fly lines come in many different shapes, each designed to soar through the air in a different way. The level line has a tip that is the exact same thickness and weight as its midsection. All the other basic types of fly lines taper to a thin front that lets anglers make "delicate presentations" so that they don't scare fish. A weight-forward line has a thin tip and a thick front and midsection that taper backward into a long, smooth, light line. The extra weight at the front of the line helps it shoot through the air faster and over greater distances.

Fly Line Weight, Density, Coating, and Color

The size of a fly line is also referred to as its weight. The weight of the line is based on the fly that will be used. Small lines are good for small flies; big lines are good for big flies. The fly size is matched to the thickness of the line, plain and simple.

The largest and lightest type of line is a floating line used for fishing with so-called "dry lines," which float on top of the water. Floating fly

Some flies are designed to imitate a specific insect, fish, or creature. Others are designed to attract fish with bright colors, enticing movement, or even mouthwatering sounds.

lines are often coated with plastic that contains air bubbles. Sometimes they are also coated with chemicals that help them float. A sink-tip fly line floats, then dives beneath the surface about 5 to 15 feet (1.5 to 4.6 m) from the tip.

A full-sinking line will sink to the bottom of the water. Different lines will sink more slowly or quickly, depending on their density and coating. Fast-sinking lines are coated with lead or similar heavy materials, like tungsten. There are also specialty coatings designed for use in different types of water or to reduce or increase line friction.

Many beginners prefer to fish with brightly colored, highly visible fly line. Strangely enough, bright fly lines don't bother most fish. But in some very clear and heavily fished waters, use of a Day-Glo orange line is to be avoided. In these cases, dark and neutral colors work best because they are less visible to fish.

Backing

What happens when an angler hooks a big fish that runs all the way to the end of his or her line? The angler should have backing, or backup line, stored in his or her reel. Even if this extra line is never needed, backing provides extra weight to balance the rod. It also fills up the reel so that the fishing line can be wound and unwound in nice, big loops—not hard-to-manage small curlicues.

The Leader and the Tippett

Fly fishing line—even its tapered tip—is fairly thick and visible. In order to properly deceive a fish, the angler wants to tie the fly to the smallest, least visible, yet strongest line that he or she can manage. A thin leader provides extra length, which improves the angler's cast and helps deceive fish into thinking that the fly is an innocent, free-floating snack. The leader tapers from the "butt," which is the same thickness as the fishing line, to the thin "tip."

In general, a leader for a floating line will be between 6 and 12 feet (1.8 and 3.6 m) long. When using a sinking line or a sink-tip line, be aware that the leader won't sink like the line does. This means that a much shorter leader should be used so that the fly bobs up to the surface.

The thin end of the leader has a tendency to wear out or break off. So some anglers repair old leaders with an extra bit of monofilament, called the tip or tippet, tied to the leader on one end and the fly on the other. Anglers fishing for sharp-toothed fish sometimes use a bite or shock tippet, made out of extra-strong material, to keep angry fish from snapping off their flies.

Fun with Flies

The most widespread and popular types of flies imitate or suggest natural fish foods. The basic rule of fly selection is this: when you arrive on the water, check out what the fish are eating and select a fly that imitates that insect (or other creature).

Aquatic Insects

Freshwater fish love to eat aquatic insects that spend part of their lives in the air and part of their lives in the water. Insects like caddis flies, mayflies, dragonflies, stoneflies, and others go through a distinctive life cycle. They may start their lives as an egg, hatch into a larva, and then develop into an aquatic "nymph" before emerging onto the water's surface as a winged, airborne adult. These adults mate and lay eggs, and then the life cycle continues. You can buy or create flies that imitate aquatic insects in every developmental phase of their lives.

Other Watery Fare

Fish consume a lot more than just aquatic insects. Big fish like to eat smaller fish, like minnows. The appearance and motion of small fish can be imitated by streamers and sliders. Fish will also happily dine on crustaceans like shrimp and crayfish, and there are wet flies that imitate these creatures, too.

Many anglers learn to make their own flies. Shown here are a few important pieces of fly tying equipment. Counterclockwise from top center are hackle pliers, a vise, a bobbin threader, and scissors.

Terrestrials

Fish will happily munch on land-dwelling insects and animals that fall into the water by mistake. Terrestrial flies imitate grasshoppers, crickets, ants, beetles, moths, bees, spiders, and even frogs and mice. These terrestrials work particularly well when there are fewer aquatic insects active on the water. Poppers, which imitate land insects and animals, pop and splash appealingly in the water. They often look delicious to bass in particular.

Homemade Flies

Many anglers enjoy making their own flies out of feathers, fur, and string. Fly tying, as this activity is called, requires special equipment, practice, and dedication. While it might initially seem impossible to create good flies at home, with a little practice anglers can become very proficient at it. Fly tiers, whether amateur or professional, come to love their craft, which can rise to the level of art. Fly tying is beyond the scope of this book, but there are plenty of fly tying classes, videos, and books out there. And there are few things in life as satisfying as fooling a fish with a fly you tied yourself!

Attractors

Attractor flies don't really imitate any specific type of fish food, but they excite and entice fish anyway. Often attractors draw the attention of fish by their bright colors or their covering of hair. Sometimes, when no other kinds of fly are working, attractors can be surprisingly effective.

Other Equipment

Fly fishers must do a lot of repairing and mending on the water. That means there are a lot of little pieces of equipment that are essential to have on hand when fly fishing. Here's a partial list of must-have tackle:

- Fly floatant: Anglers waterproof dry flies with pastes, sprays, or liquids so that they float longer.
- Hemostats: "Hemostat" is just a fancy word for forceps—small pliers that come in handy when it's time to unhook a fish. Hemostats can also be used to tie flies and tamp down barbs on fishing hooks so that it's easier to unhook and release fish.
- Clippers: Clippers are for tying and trimming knots in the fly line, leader, tippet, and other monofilament.
- Hook sharpener: Always keep your hooks sharp. A dull hook lets fish slip away.
- Camera: If you're catching and releasing fish, you'll want a souvenir of your catch. Make sure you've got a camera nice enough to take a good photo, but not so nice that you'll be heartbroken if you drop it in the water.
- Gear totes: A fly fisherman's vest or a lanyard worn around the neck will keep most vital equipment on the water, including

the fly box (where flies are stored and organized), forceps, needle, first-aid kit, and other small gear. A gear bag should be waterproof and big enough to hold rain gear, sunglasses, hat, sunblock, and a change of clothes.

Taking Care of Fishing Gear

Graphite fly fishing rods are easy to break, so they should always be stored in hard carrying cases. After every fishing trip, dry off the fly line with a paper towel. Reel it in, squeezing out and drying off the line as you go. If there are any "wind knots" in the line or leader, make sure to untangle them. These knots will weaken the line over time.

Line gets dirty and gritty over time. When that happens, it will become harder to cast. Clean the line using soap and warm water, and dry it with a soft cloth. Remember, many fishing lines are coated in plastic, so steer clear of solvents that eat through plastic. You should cut the end of your line and retie or replace the leader after a day or two of fishing. The little nicks and frays will give way, resulting in lost fish. Above all, make sure that the rod, line, and reel are completely dry before putting them away.

CHAPTER 3

Learning About Fish, Their Habitats, and Their Tendencies

The expert angler has the brain of an etymologist, the eye of a sharpshooter, the hand of a puppeteer, and the feet of a ninja. Anglers also have to learn all they can about fish, the better to fool them.

Finding Fish

Fish will be found in different places at different times of year. Every fish species has its own optimum water temperature. When the water is too cold or too hot, fish may slow down, or even die. This means that summer and winter are often slower fishing seasons. But in the fall, or the spring, when the insect hatches are out and the fish are

An angler fishes in a chilly autumn stream. Whatever season you fish in, learn exactly what insects and other creatures the fish in your water are likely to be eating and where in the water they are likely to be feeding.

feeding, there are valiant battles of wit and strength to be fought on the water between fish and angler.

If it's a hot day, fish might be found cooling off near the surface. Or they might seek out colder water, perhaps by an underground spring, because cold water carries more oxygen than warm water. If it's a cool day, the fish might feed in sunny, shallow water.

Fooling Fish

The more anglers know about how their aquatic prey see and sense the world, the better equipped they will be to catch fish. Fish see well, hear well, and have excellent senses of smell. That's why anglers have to sneak up on fish and work hard to fool them. Fish even have excellent memories. If you are on a river that hosts many anglers, the trout you're fishing for have probably become very savvy and familiar with the common tricks of anglers. You'll either have to use an extremely convincing fly or entice the trout with something unexpected.

Trout are the most iconic quarry of the fly fisherman. This rainbow trout was landed in Alaska. Note the well-equipped angler's fly vest, brightly colored fly line, hat, and polarized sunglasses.

Fly Fishing for Trout and Bass in Streams and Rivers

Fishing for trout and bass in streams and rivers is one of the most challenging—and satisfying—experiences that fly fishing has to offer. One important thing to remember is that trout and bass like to live life "on the edge." Look for fish along the edges of a stream, at the spot where a smaller stream joins a river, where a stream becomes a pool, or a pool becomes a creek.

Creeks, streams, and rivers are filled with moving water. This means that simply swimming along in the current, looking for food, requires the expenditure of a certain amount of energy from a fish. Trout like to find spots where they can rest in calmer water. One favorite fish spot is the pocket water behind a boulder. Trout love to rest in this relatively calm water while their food is brought to them by the faster currents rushing by. Fish also like to hang out by the edges of the stream, underneath under-cut banks, in a back eddy, by an underwater ledge or drop-off, or by the seam where two different speeds or types of water converge. Riffles and midstream obstructions also promise good fishing.

Try to "match the hatch" by choosing a dry fly that looks like the insects currently populating the stream where you're fishing. During the summer, when there's lots of fish food on the water, trout can be very selective and may focus on eating just one type of food. Take some time to closely observe the insects as they behave in nature and upon the water. If an insect is moving in a certain way, try to move your fly in the exact same manner. If most of the insects on the water's surface are already dead (or at least not moving), don't move your fly. Let the current carry it along naturally. Otherwise, you run the risk of making your fish suspicious. Many wet flies used on streams and rivers are designed to imitate or suggest nymphs, or the water-bound phase of aquatic insects. Nymphs can float just beneath the surface or can go to the bottom of the water, and so, too, can flies designed to imitate them, especially with the help of a sink tip or sinking line.

Fish have excellent senses of smell, so make sure to brush or rub the wet fly against moss or stream rocks to give it a watery smell before your first cast. When using a streamer to imitate a small fish, you'll usually want to use a sink tip or sinking line to dive under the water's surface. You can entice your fish with a streamer by playing hard to get—swim your streamer away from your quarry. Give your streamer an unpredictable pattern of swimming and stopping, similar to the motions of a weak, vulnerable minnow. Or try fishing a streamer without moving it at all—let the current move it, and allow the fish to think that it's about to snap up a small dead fish for a snack.

If you use a "bug" (a fly that imitates a frog, mouse, or other terrestrial) in moving water, you're trying to fool your fish into thinking it has spotted a land creature in the process of drowning. Let the fly get swept away with the current and "puppeteer" it so that it appears to be struggling to the water's surface. This type of presentation will be most convincing near the shore, where land critters sometimes fall into the water.

Fishing for Trout, Bass, and Panfish in Ponds and Lakes

Once again, look along the edges of the water. Bass and trout alike tend to hang out around underwater structures, particularly spots that promise a meal. Rock piles beneath the water's surface are often crayfish condominiums and, therefore, favorite snack spots for bass. Underwater brush piles, stumps, moss, and weed beds will attract fish.

A largemouth bass is measured against a fishing rod. Bass can grow large, so bass fishing rods are often bigger and sturdier than trout rods.

Fish also like to cruise flats and points. Underwater springs and inlets of cold spring water rushing into a lake or pond will draw fish on sweltering summer days. Also look for underwater stream channels at the bottom of a pond or lake. These areas are often popular with trout.

Bass

Bass are creatures of habit that often prefer to stick to the same types of environments at the same time of day. If a line cast out onto a lake flat at dawn attracts lots of fish, chances are that similar flats on that lake should also yield some good fishing at dawn.

Saltwater Fishing

Many dedicated anglers enjoy fly fishing in salt water. Anglers can catch saltwater fish on the beach, on a saltwater flat, or on a tidal river. Saltwater fish are usually smarter, quicker, and stronger than freshwater fish—and they are very exciting to battle. Some popular saltwater species are striped bass, tarpon, bonefish, redfish, bluefish, weakfish, snook, and even barracuda.

Because saltwater fish are bigger and tougher, they take bigger flies. Plus, saltwater anglers often have to contend with strong coastal winds. Consequently, a saltwater tackle is usually bigger, stronger and more difficult to handle than other fly fishing equipment.

Trout are often picky eaters, but bass are more adventurous. They enjoy flashy attractors and are intrigued, not spooked, by flies that plop into the water with a splash. Bass flies are bigger and glitzier than trout flies. Bass love poppers—flies designed to pop up and down in the water, bubbling and gurgling. They also chase streamers, such as sliders, that imitate small minnows.

Bass are attracted by erratic movements. When the fly lands in the water, let it sit for a while, and then start to manipulate it, giving it a nice lifelike motion and feel. Experiment until you find a rhythm the bass can't resist.

Panfish

There's a wide world of freshwater fishing out there beyond just trout and bass. Panfish, also called bream, are small, pan-sized fish in the

Many panfish, like this bluegill, have small mouths and therefore must be caught with small, delicate tackle.

sunfish, perch, and bass families. They cluster near streamside foliage and aquatic plants such as lily pads and weed beds. Just like bass, they adore underwater structures such as piers and bridge supports. They travel in schools, so where one panfish is found, there will probably be others.

Here are some common panfish to keep an eye out for in backyard ponds or in creeks, streams, and other slow-moving water:

- Bluegill are small and feisty members of the sunfish family. They eat a range of food—from crustaceans and smaller fish to insects—but they have tiny mouths. Use lighter trout tackle to fish for them.

- Crappies like the same types of food as bluegills but are especially fond of minnows. They like to hide near, under, or inside underwater objects.
- Perch feed on the bottom, or below the surface. Besides nymphs, minnows, and crustaceans, they like worms and leeches. They adore bright things that move erratically.

Be aware that panfish have spiny fins on their backs. If you try to grab them unprepared, you could be in for a painful surprise. Use your finger to smooth their top fin down, from the head to the tail, before you grab hold of them.

CHAPTER 4

FLY CASTING

So you've got your tackle together, and you know how to find your fish. Just how do you cast your fly out onto the water, anyway? First of all, fly fishing isn't a matter of casting the fly over the water. It's actually a matter of casting the line. An effective cast will move the weighted fly line through the air so that it unravels over the water in a straight line. The rod is designed to help the angler direct the line accurately toward a specific target. The line follows the rod tip. If the angler builds up momentum and then suddenly stops the rod, the line will continue moving in the direction that the rod's tip is pointing.

The Mechanics of Fly Casting

In order to learn how to cast, many fly anglers

Casting a line takes skill and practice, just like learning to shoot a basket or hit a baseball. But you can save yourself hours of frustration if you understand the basic mechanics and motion of a fly fishing cast.

imagine themselves standing in the center of a clock, with their head at twelve o'clock and their feet at six. If the hand is held straight out in front, it would be at nine o'clock.

Having visualized the body's position as hours on a clock, the next step is to pick up the line. It is vitally important to get the whole line moving, from the rod tip to the end of the line. To begin the pickup, start with the rod tip low, pointed toward the water. Pick it up at a moderate speed, to ten o'clock. When the rod tip reaches ten o'clock, start to move the rod more quickly. The higher the rod gets, the quicker it should move. Then snap to a stop exactly at twelve o'clock. This sudden stop will create momentum and send the line flying out behind you in a straight line. As it straightens, the line should create a tight, controllable loop. The art of casting is the art of forming tight loops that will help the angler direct and shoot the line.

Pause as the line straightens out behind you. Beginners might want to turn their heads and watch for the ideal moment to start the next part of their cast: right as the fly line has almost stretched straight out behind them. The line should be shaped like a candy cane—straight with a short hook at the end.

Now it's time to perform the opposite of the back cast. Flip it and reverse it: bring the line down and forward from twelve to ten o'clock, speeding up as you go. Remember, acceleration, not speed, is the key to a good cast. Stop right at ten o'clock. Once again, the abrupt stop will create momentum. The fly line should unfurl in another tight loop, sending it straight forward. Less power can be used on the forward cast because gravity is on your side. Imagine you're hammering a small, light nail into a wall.

As the line falls, lower it toward the water slowly and gently. Let gravity do its thing. The leader and fly will follow. The line should land lightly in a straight line on the water. If the line makes a big splash, you've moved your arm too much or used too much power, creating a wide loop.

Holding the Rod

The most standard rod grip is to put the thumb on top of the rod and wrap the other fingers firmly, but not tightly, around the side of the rod. If the fingers turn white when holding the rod, the angler is squeezing too hard. A death grip will make it difficult to cast well.

Wide loops result in clumsy landings. There is less force and more art to the business of casting than most beginning anglers imagine.

When the line is on the water, grip it with the right index finger, keeping hold of the line in case a fish takes it immediately. If some line needs to be pulled in to reduce slack, strip it back with your left hand instead of using the reel.

Practice Makes Perfect

To practice a regular overhead cast, you should have lots of room behind and all around you. It's good to do this on a calm water surface, not a flowing stream or brook. But a gymnasium floor or a well-mowed lawn will also work. Use a hookless fly, a practice fly, or just tie a bit of yarn to the end of the leader.

Strip about 30 to 35 feet (9 to 10 m) of line off the reel. Pull the fly, leader, and line through the rod guides, and stretch the line out as straight as possible in front of you. Stand with your feet shoulder-width apart. The hand that you write with will be your casting hand. Stand with your casting foot slightly backward.

Now try to cast. Then try again, and again, and again. Some beginners find it helpful to aim at some specific target, like a bottle or a

Start out by practicing your cast on a field or on a smooth surface. Practice makes perfect when it comes to learning how to cast tight loops.

Frisbee placed on the ground. Remember, the clock positions are guide-lines, not rules. Practice and experiment to find a casting rhythm and method that works best for you.

Many teachers recommend practicing casting from side to side so that you can experiment with different angles, speeds, and amounts of force. Angled casting may be necessary if you have little room behind you, if there are overhead obstructions like tree branches, or there are high winds. Observe the loops that different casting methods create in the line. Waving the fly line back and forth overhead can also be prac-ticed; this is called false casting. It is often used to shake water off the line and fly.

This angler is casting upstream. When his cast lands, the current will move his fly in a natural and enticing manner through the rushing water. It will eventually drift downstream right back to him.

If at all possible, take some fly casting lessons from an expert angler and/or watch instructional fly casting videos.

More Casts

There are many other casts to learn. Some will be useful on any fishing trip, and some are intended for specific or sticky situations. When there's no room behind or above you to make a normal cast, use a roll cast. This is like a normal cast performed without throwing the line backward and overhead. The roll cast is also helpful for straightening out the line, repositioning it on moving water, or casting when there are strong winds. Hold the fly rod out in front of you and make sure there are no tangles in your fly line. Bring the fly rod tip back so that a small portion of line hangs loosely behind your casting shoulder. Move the fly rod forward slowly at first, then accelerate steadily. Stop when the rod tip is still pointing slightly upward and watch the loop unroll.

Sidearm casting is like regular casting turned on its side. This is useful when there are long hanging branches overhead or when an angler wants to sneak up on a fish. Sometimes an angler might curve the line in midair during a regular cast, creating a curve cast. This cast helps lay the line out in a curve shape on the water—a handy cast when trying to avoid a boulder midstream.

If you stick with fly fishing, you'll learn all these casts and more. Maybe you'll even invent a few of your own!

CHAPTER 5

CATCHING FISH

So you've learned some fly fishing casting techniques, and you've finally hooked a fish. Playing and landing your catch takes just as much skill as enticing a fish to take your fly.

Setting the Hook

Sometimes fish strike near the surface and make a big splash. But if the fly is beneath the surface, it might not be easy to tell whether a fish has swallowed it. Watch the water carefully for unnatural or unexpected movements. You might feel, or even hear, a strike before you see it. Some wet fly fishermen use bright strike indicators to make fish strikes more obvious.

If you suspect a hit, wait a brief moment to make sure the fish took your fly—and then take decisive action. You've got to set the hook deep

Some fish have sharp teeth, but not bass. You can reach into their mouths and take out your hook without any fear of being cut.

into the fish's mouth. Otherwise, the fish could spit it out and flee. It's easy to set a small fly by pulling up and back. Make sure you are holding the line firmly. A small, sharp, barbless hook should penetrate the fish's mouth smoothly and efficiently. The fish will naturally try to break free. Keep the rod at a forty-five-degree angle to the water to absorb the pressure as the fish fights you. Keep an eye on the rod and line—the line and leader should be taut but not strained. If the fish is fighting hard, you can give it a little slack. Just don't let the line go loose.

When fishing with a bigger fly, a slightly different technique is needed. When you feel a fish strike, take in some of the slack from the line. You might need to tug: this force is necessary to set the hook. Then lower the rod's tip down toward the water, more level than raised. Pull backward on the rod's butt. Both the rod angle and the backward motion help hook the fish firmly. Reel in some of the slack—if slack is pulled in only by hand, the line might get tangled.

Bringing the Fish In

When fishing in a stream or river, make the current your friend. Stand downstream from your catch or pull it in across the current. When trying to reel in a fish that the water is pushing downstream, you're fighting both the fish and the current.

Keep fighting the fish until you are absolutely sure that it is good and tired. It'll be easier to land the catch, and you can be sure the fish won't try to make a last-minute getaway. When the fish appears to be thoroughly worn out, keep pulling in line until the line is about the same length as the rod. It's unnecessary to pull a fish all the way up to the tip of the rod.

Catch-and-Release

These days, a lot of anglers prefer to release their catches. The more fish that are released back into the water, the more fish there will be for the next angler to catch. Plus, there will be more fish to spawn the next generation.

A caught fish can be released without the angler ever having to touch it (and possibly harm or injure it unintentionally). Pull on the line and leader, then use a hemostat to twist the hook out of the fish's mouth.

Releasing a fish is not always so simple, however. The angler may need to grab hold of the fish, use a landing net, or bring the fish up onto a shallow beach. In every one of these cases, be careful to release the fish without harming it.

Catch-and-release was popularized in North America by famous angler, teacher, author, and wildlife advocate Lee Wulff. He argued that catch-and-release could help preserve threatened fish species. Today, many fishing spots, like this one on the Wisconsin River, require catch-and-release.

Bass have hard jaws but no sharp teeth. If you land a bass, you can stick your fingers inside its mouth and hold it up by the jaw as you twist your hook free. This is also a great hold for photographing bass, as long as the fish isn't kept out of the water for too long. This strategy should never be used with trout, which have delicate, easily damaged jaws.

Fish like pike and gar have sharp teeth, so their bodies, not their jaws, must be grabbed. Remember to wet your hands before handling any fish. Fish are covered in protective slime, and dry hands can hurt them. Be gentle and careful whenever handling a live fish. Don't squeeze a fish around the middle, as this could damage its organs. And whatever you do, never stick your fingers inside a fish's gills.

Reviving a Fish

Never throw a fish back in the water without reviving it. To revive a fish, cradle it upright in clean water. If you're in a stream, face upstream so that the water pumps naturally through the fish's gills. If it's a hot day, try to revive the fish in cooler, more oxygenated water. Releasing a fish into more sheltered water increases its chances of success. Tossing a tired fish into whitewater can be a death sentence. When the fish is properly revived, it should swim right out of your hands.

A fisherman prepares to revive a steelhead on British Columbia's Bulkley River.

When attempting to "beach" a fish in shallow water, make sure that it is thoroughly tired out first. Bring the fish onto a smooth surface—no rocks, sticks, or gravel. Let the line relax, photograph the fish, and unhook it. The fish might need to be eased gently back into deeper water.

If using a landing net, be aware that certain net materials harm fish skin. Cotton and nylon nets are fine for fish you plan to keep, but they'll be rough on any fish you'd like to release. When catching and releasing fish, use a soft rubber net.

If a fish has been hooked in the throat or side, it's better to cut off the leader and leave the hook in place. And remember, exhausted fish are less likely to survive. Tire the fish out before landing it, but don't work it to death.

Catch-and-Keep

If you're planning to keep your catch, it becomes even more important to thoroughly tire the fish out before taking it out of the water. Once the fish is out of the water, it's kinder to kill it quickly than to let it gasp painfully. Remove the hook, and then hit it hard behind the eyes or on the very top of its head.

Wild Fish and Health Concerns

As exciting as it is to catch a fish and eat it streamside, a note of caution must be sounded. Unfortunately, many North American waterways are contaminated with mercury, chemicals like PCBs, and even heavy metals such as arsenic and lead. Fish naturally accumulate these chemicals within their bodies. That means that it might not be safe for anglers to eat everything they take out of the water.

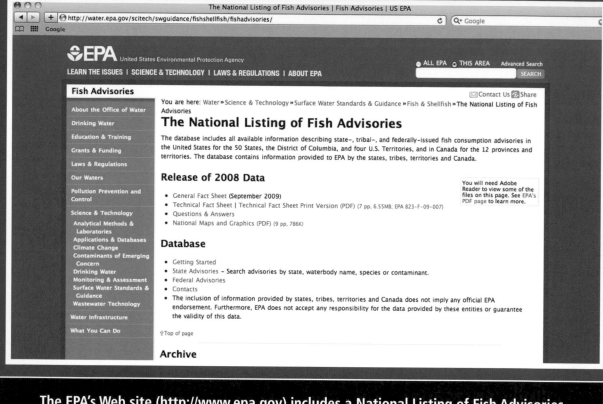

The EPA's Web site (http://www.epa.gov) includes a National Listing of Fish Advisories. These days, it's wise to check such listings to see whether the fish that you've caught are safe to eat.

If you're planning to keep some fish, take a moment to check local fish and waterway advisories through the Environmental Protection Agency (EPA). You might be surprised by what you find out. For instance, in much of upstate New York, children under fifteen and women under fifty (women of childbearing age) should not eat the fish they catch because of the high levels of mercury and other chemicals present in the fish.

The Food and Drug Administration (FDA) recommends that, in general, a person should not eat any more than one meal per week of fish that was caught by himself or herself. He or she should also avoid consuming other fish during that one-week period after eating a self-caught fish.

CHAPTER 6

THE ETHICAL ANGLER

t is important that anglers do all they can to preserve the glorious fishing habitats they enjoy so much. A fisherman or fisherwoman who acts courteously to others and leaves the environment better for future generations is called an ethical angler.

Being Responsible and Law-Abiding

The ethical angler takes pride in following local laws and regulations, including fishing seasons, size limits, and daily limits. If you observe violations of local fishing laws, don't be afraid to report them to the authorities. Never take more fish than needed or truly wanted out of the water.

It's important to take good care of fishing sites.

Sometimes you'll find waters polluted by accident—like this riverside littered with trash after a big rainstorm—or by human carelessness and negligence. Always try to leave your fishing spot cleaner than you found it, even if that means cleaning up other people's messes.

This means never litter and always pack out everything that has been packed in. Don't dump fuel from a boat, either into the water or onto land. Don't leave any trace of your presence by the water, and clean up any messes left by unethical anglers.

Show respect for the private property of others when fishing. If you want to fish on private land, always ask permission and never trespass. When fishing a stream with other anglers, give them space. Don't crowd into the water; wait your turn to fish. When another angler is landing a fish, you should stop fishing. That's just polite. Try to treat other anglers with generosity, respect, and consideration— the same way that you would like to be treated.

Future Generations

If we don't take care of our environment, our children and grandchildren might not enjoy the fishing opportunities we do. Learn about organizations like Trout Unlimited, which attempts to preserve fishing habitats for future generations. Trout Unlimited supports new scientific studies, lobbies for new conservation laws, and mobilizes volunteers to improve fishing ecosystems. The advocacy of anglers, individually and collectively, can really make a huge difference.

Always ask permission before casting your line on private property. If a NO FISHING sign is posted, respect the landowner's wishes and rights.

There's something else any and all anglers can do to help preserve our great waterways: introduce friends or younger family members to fishing. Teach them how to fish ethically and responsibly. Inspire them to get involved. If more people fall in love with fly fishing, more people will have a stake in the health and future viability of North America's natural resources. There will be more voices speaking out for the protection, preservation, and restoration of our waterways for generations to come.

algae An organism that can appear much like an aquatic plant. Algae may take many forms, but fishermen often encounter it as green or brown slime coating rocks or other underwater structures.

angler Another word for a fisherman, specifically one who fishes with a line and hook.

caddis fly A small, mothlike insect that lives part of its life in water and part of its life flying around water. Caddis flies are one of the main insect forms of fish food on streams and rivers.

cast The act of sending a fishing line through the air.

catch-and-release A fishing technique practiced by anglers concerned with conservation. After catching a fish, the angler releases it alive and unharmed into the water, taking care that the fish recovers.

crappie Two separate species of small sunfish that live in fresh water.

crayfish Small crustaceans, often found in fresh water, that look a little bit like clawless lobsters.

crustacean An animal with a hard shell, antennae, and no backbone that usually lives in the water.

drag Friction that keeps the reel from turning easily, thereby helping the angler tire out hooked fish.

dry fly A type of lure for fish designed to float on the water's surface.

ecosystem The way in which animals, plants, and other organisms in a given place interact with each other and the natural environment to create a stable living community.

eddy An area in a body of moving water in which the water swirls in a circle or flows in a manner different from the main current.

Environmental Protection Agency (EPA) The EPA is a government agency charged with regulating and protecting the environment.

ethics The philosophy of right and wrong, as expressed in society's commonly accepted morals and values.

fly tying The art of creating artificial fly fishing lures, or flies, for fishing, using feathers, string, fur, and other materials.

gar A type of primitive fish with long jaws, dangerous teeth, and hard scales.

hemostat Pliers used in fly fishing for tying knots, creating flies, tamping down barbs, and releasing hooked fish.

landing net A handled fish net used for landing fish and lifting them out of the water.

larva In the insect life cycle, the larva is a stage between egg and maturity.

mercury A metallic element that is found in many bodies of water and accumulates in the bodies of fish. Mercury is toxic and can be dangerous to humans if consumed in too great a quantity.

microorganism An organism (living creature) too small to be seen without a microscope.

monofilament A very thin wire, fiber, or thread. Monofilament is used to tie flies to fishing lines as invisibly as possible.

nymph A phase of insect development just before adulthood. Nymphs appear similar to adult insects but without fully developed, and hence functional, wings.

panfish Many different types of delicious, edible fish that fit easily into a frying pan.

PCB Polychlorinated biphenyl, a type of toxic chemical once commonly used to create electricity and electrical equipment, as well as in other products and processes. It is now recognized as toxic. PCBs pollute many waterways.

pike The American name for a common, carnivorous, ferocious fish found in fresh water and brackish (mixed salt and fresh) water.

pocket water In rough or rushing water, an area of calm water behind large midstream obstacles, such as rocks and boulders. Many fish enjoy resting in pocket water.

popper A type of fly designed to float along the surface of water, making a pop or gurgle as it moves.

quarry A hunter or angler's prey.

riffle A stretch of fast-moving current tumbling over an uneven stream or river bed, creating a series of small waves.

roll cast One of the most useful casts, basically a modified forward cast in which the line does not fly out behind the angler. The roll cast has many uses, including casting when there are obstacles behind the angler, preventing a back cast.

steelhead A rainbow trout that migrates from salt water to fresh water in order to spawn; a prized fish much sought after by fly anglers.

stone fly An aquatic insect with a flat body and wings, imitated by fly anglers in all of its life phases.

sunfish A category of flat, carnivorous freshwater fish, including pumpkinseed and bluegills.

tippet Thin monofilament connecting the leader to the fly.

wet fly A type of fly designed to sink and attract fish beneath the water's surface.

American Angler Magazine
P.O. Box 34
Boulder, CO 80329-0034
(800) 877-5305
Web site: http://www.americanangler.com
American Angler provides solid how-to information for those seek-
ing to master fly fishing—the most sophisticated of angling sports.
Articles written by well-known experts and laymen alike cover every
region, technique, and species of fish that can be taken on a fly.

American Museum of Fly Fishing
4104 Main Street
Manchester, VT 05354
(802) 362-3300
Web site: http://www.amff.com
The American Museum of Fly Fishing promotes an understanding of
and appreciation for the history, traditions, and practitioners of the
sport of fly fishing.

Federation of Fly Fishers
P.O. Box 1688
Livingston, MT 59047
(406) 222-9369
Web site: http://www.fedflyfishers.org
The Federation of Fly Fishers is an international nonprofit organi-
zation dedicated to the betterment of the sport of fly fishing
through conservation, restoration, and education.

FishAmerica Foundation
225 Reinekers Lane, Suite 420

Alexandria, VA 22314

(703) 519-9691

Web site: http://www.fishamerica.org

The FishAmerica Foundation is the conservation and research foundation of the American Sportfishing Association. It strives to keep the nation's fish and waters healthy.

L. L. Bean Fly-Fishing School

L. L. Bean, Inc.

Freeport, ME 04033-0001

(888) LLB-EAN1 [552-3261]

Web site: http://www.llbean.com/outdoorsOnline/odp/courses/ flyfishingcourses/index.html

L. L. Bean's Fly-Fishing School allows anglers at all levels to select the courses, private lessons, or guided fishing trips suitable to their skills and interests.

Orvis Fly-Fishing Schools

4180 Main Street

Manchester, VT 05254

(802) 362-4604

Web site: http://www.orvis.com/store/product_directory_tnail.aspx?dir_ id=19730&group_id=19731&cat_id=19732&subcat_id=19733

Orvis's flagship fly-fishing school in Manchester, Vermont, is the premier school dedicated to fly fishing in the country. There are other schools in Oregon, Tennessee, California, New York, Missouri, Colorado, Pennsylvania, Michigan, Virginia, Idaho, and Florida. Students will learn the skills necessary to fly fish anywhere in the world.

Trout Unlimited
1300 North 17th Street, Suite 500
Arlington, VA 22209-2404
(800) 834-2419
Web site: http://www.tu.org
Trout Unlimited is dedicated to the conservation, protection, and restoration of North America's coldwater fisheries and their watersheds.

U.S. Fish and Wildlife Service
1849 C Street NW
Washington, DC 20240
(800) 344-WILD [9453]
Web site: http://www.fws.gov
The U.S. Fish and Wildlife Service's mission is to work with others to conserve, protect, and enhance fish, wildlife, and plants and their habitats for the continuing benefit of the American people.

Web Sites

Due to the changing nature of Internet links, Rosen Publishing has developed an online list of Web sites related to the subject of this book. This site is updated regularly. Please use this link to access the list:

http://www.rosenlinks.com/fish/fly

Hellekson, Terry. *Fish Flies: The Encyclopedia of the Fly Tier's Art.* Layton, UT: Gibbs Smith, 2005.

Hughes, Dave. *Handbook of Hatches: Introductory Guide to the Foods Trout Eat & the Most Effective Flies to Match Them.* Mechanicsburg, PA: Stackpole Books, 2005.

Kaminsky, Peter. *The Fly Fisherman's Guide to the Meaning of Life.* New York, NY: Skyhorse Publishing, 2008.

Macauley, Lord, et al. *The L. L. Bean Ultimate Book of Fly Fishing.* Guilford, CT: The Lyons Press, 2006.

McClintock, Grant. *Flywater: Fly-Fishing Rivers of the West.* New York, NY: Universe, 2010.

Meck, Charles. *Fishing Tandem Flies: Tactics, Techniques, and Rigs to Catch More Trout.* New Cumberland, PA: Headwater Books, 2007.

Meyers, Charlie, and Kirk Deeter. *The Little Red Book of Fly Fishing.* New York, NY: Skyhorse Publishing, 2010.

Nichols, Jay, ed. *1001 Fly Fishing Tips: Expert Advice, Hints, and Shortcuts from the World's Leading Fly Fishers.* New Cumberland, PA: Headwater Books, 2008.

Quigley, Ed. *Fly Fishing Advice from an Old Timer: A Practical Guide to the Sport and Its Language.* Bloomington, IN: iUniverse, 2009.

Rosenbauer, Tom. *The Orvis Fly-Fishing Guide.* Guilford, CT: The Lyons Press, 2007.

Rosenbauer, Tom. *The Orvis Guide to Beginning Fly Fishing: 101 Tips for the Absolute Beginner.* New York, NY: Skyhorse Publishing, 2009.

Rosenbauer, Tom. *The Orvis Ultimate Book of Fly Fishing: Secrets from the Orvis Experts.* Guilford, CT: The Lyons Press, 2005.

Rosenbauer, Tom. *The Orvis Vest Pocket Guide to Leaders, Knots, and Tippets: A Detailed Field Guide to Leader Construction,*

Fly-Fishing Knots, Tippets, and More. Guilford, CT: The Lyons Press, 2008.

Schullery, Paul. *The Rise: Streamside Observations on Trout, Flies, and Fly Fishing*. Mechanicsburg, PA: Stackpole Books, 2006.

Shook, Michael D. *The Complete Idiot's Guide to Fly Fishing*. New York, NY: Alpha, 2005.

Sousa, Robert J. *Learn to Fly Fish in 24 Hours*. New York, NY: Ragged Mountain Press. 2007.

Whitlock, Dave. *Trout and Their Food: A Compact Guide for Fly Fishers*. New York, NY: Skyhorse Publishing, 2010.

BIBLIOGRAPHY

Combs, Trey. *Steelhead Fly Fishing*. Guilford, CT: The Lyons Press, 1991.

Craven, Charlie. *Charlie Craven's Basic Fly Tying*. New Cumberland, PA: Headwater Books, 2008.

Ellis, Jack. *Bassin' with a Fly Rod: One Fly Rodder's Approach to Serious Bass Fishing*. Guilford, CT: The Lyons Press, 2003.

Hughes, Dave. *Strategies for Stillwater: The Tackle, Techniques, and Flies for Taking Trout in Lakes and Ponds*. Mechanicsburg, PA: Stackpole Books, 1991.

Jawarowski, Ed. *The Cast*. Mechanicsburg, PA: Stackpole Books, 1992.

Kreh, Lefty. *Fly Casting with Lefty Kreh*. Waukesha, WI: Tomorrow River Press, 1992.

Kugach, Gene. *Fishing Tips for Freshwater*. Mechanicsburg, PA: Stackpole Books, 2002.

MacLean, Norman. *A River Runs Through It: And Other Stories*. Chicago, IL: The University of Chicago Press, 2001.

Merwin, John. *Fly Fishing, A Trailside Guide*. New York, NY: W. W. Norton & Company, 1996.

Merwin, John. *The New American Trout Fishing*. New York, NY: Macmillan General Reference, 1997.

Morris, Skip. *Fly Tying Made Clear and Simple*. Portland, OR: Frank Amato Publications, 1992.

Notley, Larry V. *Guide to Fly Fishing Knots: A Basic Streamside Guide for Fly Fishing Knots, Tippets, and Leader Formulas*. Portland, OR: Frank Amato Publications, 1999.

Price, Steven D. *The Ultimate Fishing Guide*. New York, NY: HarperCollins, 1996.

Randolph, John. "Why Fly Fish?" Fly Fisherman. Retrieved October 2010 (http://www.flyfisherman.com/content/why-fly-fish).

Schwiebert, Ernest. *Marching the Hatch: A Practical Guide to Imitation of Insects Found on Eastern and Western Trout Waters*. New York, NY: Macmillan, 1972.

Sosin, Mark. *Practical Saltwater Fly Fishing*. Guilford, CT: The Lyons Press, 1989.

Swisher, Doug, and Carl Richards. *Fly-Fishing Strategy*. Guilford, CT: The Lyons Press, 1975.

Tapply, William G. *Gone Fishin: Ruminations on Fly Fishing*. Guilford, CT: The Lyons Press, 2004.

Vachon, E. L. *The Simple Art of Fly Fishing*. Cold Spring Harbor, NY: Cold Spring Press, 2003.

Wulff, Joan. *Joan Wulff's Fly Fishing: Expert Advice from a Woman's Perspective*. Mechanicsburg, PA: Stackpole Books, 1991.

INDEX

About the Author

Sally Crockett is an educator, author, and aspiring sportswoman. She enjoys working with young people, reading about the natural world, and improving her knowledge of fly fishing, which has been a tradition in her family for generations. She lives in Brooklyn, New York.

About the Consultant

Contributor Benjamin Cowan has more than twenty years of both fresh and saltwater angling experience. In addition to being an avid outdoorsman, Cowan is also a member of many conservation organizations. He currently resides in west Tennessee.

Photo Credits

Designer: Nicole Russo; Photo Researcher: Peter Tomlinson